The Puzzle Of The Cross

**Sermons and Orders of Service
for Lent and Maundy Thursday**
By Elmer E. Burrall

C.S.S. Publishing Co.
Lima, Ohio

THE PUZZLE OF THE CROSS:
SERMONS FOR LENT AND MAUNDY THURSDAY

Copyright © 1991 by
The C.S.S. Publishing Company, Inc.
Lima, Ohio

9111 / ISBN 1-55673-278-3

Dedicated to the people of Christ Lutheran Church, Hot Springs Village, Arkansas, and to my wife, Kay, for her support and help.

Table of Contents

Introduction

The Puzzle Of The Cross

Let us begin our series, the puzzle of the cross with the topic of God. Have you ever had the experience of talking about someone while that person is listening? That's what happens with God. God is the unseen listener to every conversation. It is something to think about.

One of the things that makes many of us uncomfortable is silence. We want at least some bit of noise around us.

There is a poem by Clinton Scollard titled "The Great Voice." Part of which states,

> *I who have heard the solemnities of sound —*
> *The throbbing pulse of cities, the loud roar*
> *Of ocean on sheer ledges of gaunt rock,*
> *The chanting of innumerable winds*
> *Around white peaks, the plunge of cataracts,*
> *The whelm of avalanches, and, by night,*
> *The thunder of panic's breath — have come to know*
> *What is earth's mightiest voice — the desert's voice —*
> *Silence, that speaks with the deafening tones of God.*

Meister Eckhardt, a 13th century mystic, wrote "Nothing in all creation is so like God than silence."

You will note in your bulletin that we have provided places following each lesson for silent meditation. Perhaps these spaces will seem uncomfortable to us at first. We're not used to silence in our worship. Let us listen meditatively to each lesson and then spend that time in silence echoing those words in our minds while we turn our hearts to God in prayer. I will end each period of silence with the words, "Hear our prayer, O Lord. Amen."

Lent 1 — Order of Service

THE PUZZLE OF THE CROSS — GOD

Prelude

Call to Worship

Opening Hymn: "Immortal, Invisible"

Introducing the theme

Psalm 19 (Read Antiphonally)

The First Lesson: Exodus 3:1-6, 13-15

Silent Meditation

The Second Lesson: Romans 11:33-36

Silent Meditation

*The Holy Gospel: John 17:1-6

Silent Meditation

The Sermon: "The Puzzle of the Cross — God"

Sermon Hymn: "My God How Wonderful Thou Art"

The Offering and Offertory

*Congregational Offertory: The Doxology

*The Athanasian Creed

*Prayer and Lord's Prayer

*Closing Hymn: "Before Jehovah's Awesome Throne"

*Benediction

Postlude

*Congregation please stand

1 — God

The Puzzle Of The Cross — Piece Number 1

It is such a common sight. We see it everywhere — in front of, inside of, and on top of churches; hanging around the necks of all kinds of people — pastors and priests, genteel ladies and gyrating rock stars. We see it made out of every kind of material — wood, iron, brass, stone, gold, silver, precious stones. It is, of course, the cross, an ancient form of horrible torture and death which has become the symbol of Christianity.

Yet, to many it is still a puzzle. What happened on the cross almost 2,000 years ago is still a puzzle. A man named Jesus of Nazareth died on a cross. Or was he just a man? What does that event which happened so long ago mean in our lives? How could something that happened so long ago have such an effect on the world and on us? As the king of Siam said of life, "It's a puzzlement."

For the next five Wednesdays and for Maundy Thursday in Holy Week we are going to consider pieces of the puzzle of the cross. As you leave this evening, you are invited to take with you a puzzle base like this. *(Show)* On it there is an outline of a cross. We request you take only one per family unit. Each Wednesday you will receive a piece of the puzzle. The large display in the narthex and the bulletin cover each Wednesday will show you where that piece of the puzzle fits. You may fasten the puzzle piece into place at home. The back of each puzzle piece has a peel-off paper covering a pre-applied adhesive.

Should others join us on subsequent Wednesdays, or should you be unable to be with us for any particular Wednesday, additional pieces of the puzzle will be available. All you have to do is present yourself in sackcloth and ashes and get down on your knees and beg for the pieces you need. Just kidding, of course.

You will have noticed that the first piece of the puzzle is the one marked "God." You will also have noted that the piece forms the upper section of the cross. That is the proper place for it, for God is central to the puzzle of the cross, and the cross is central to the puzzle of God.

I'm not sure whether I envy or pity anyone who has never wrestled with the person of God. God is such a puzzle. We cannot see God. We see a universe around us. We poke at it, test it, probe it, seek to learn its origin, are overwhelmed by its complexity and magnitude, and posit that some Power, some Ground of Being, some First Cause had to be the Creator. This God is beyond our comprehension. We can only deal with persons and things that are finite, temporal, tangible. How can we conceive or know a Being, a Person, One who is the wholly Other: Hindus claim that because God is beyond our knowing, God has no attributes. God is simply Brahma, the creator, the unapproachable, the unknowable. Other religions attribute to God the qualities of omniscience, omnipotence, and omnipresence. And that's where the puzzle begins. If God is all-powerful, all-knowing, all-good, always present, why is the world in such an observable mess? Why is there evil in the world? Why do people suffer and die? Why doesn't God reveal himself and do something?

Christianity proclaims that God did something. God became incarnate. He took upon himself "the likeness of humanity." And God died on the cross in the person of Jesus Christ.

It's still a puzzlement. Luther said, as he meditated on the first verse of Psalm 22, "My God, my God, why hast Thou forsaken me?" Luther exclaimed, "God forsake God? How can this be?"

The church has struggled with the puzzle of God for centuries. It has formulated creeds that affirm its faith, but it has not solved the puzzle. We will shortly confess our faith by reading a creed we seldom use, the Athanasian Creed. "Shortly" is not the word for it. It is a long, confusing statement of our faith that still leaves the puzzle in place.

11

The truth is that we can never know God completely. We cannot put God in a box, or place God within the bounds of a piece of a puzzle. We can only know God to the extent that God chooses to reveal himself to us.

One aspect of that revelation is what we call the theology of the cross. Carl Braaten, a professor at the Lutheran School of Theology at Chicago, in his book, *The Apostolic Imperative*, has some pertinent thoughts about God and the puzzle of the cross. Let me quote a few of them for you:

"Only theology shaped by the cross leads to the true knowledge of the God who is really God. God can be known only in the cross and suffering, in the cross of Christ and the cross of self. In the cross of Christ we find the revelation of the hidden God. Christian faith must speak of no other God than the incarnate God, the human God, the crucified God, because God's humanity is the only means of access to God's divinity. Jesus, the crucified Christ, sheds light on the identity and meaning of God. The theology of the cross must be the doctrine of the Trinity and the doctrine of the Trinity must be the theology of the cross, because otherwise the human crucified God cannot be fully perceived. For Luther, the hidden God is the God hidden in the suffering and the cross. We should not try to penetrate the mysteries of God's majesty, but should be content with the God on the cross. We cannot find God except in Christ. Anyone who tries to find him outside Christ will find the devil."

Those are some powerful thoughts. We are so flippant with God in our lives. How often do we hear the name of God taken in vain? How often have we heard God referred to as "the man upstairs?" God is not simply an overgrown man, some old, gray-bearded person who sits on his throne in heaven. God is God. God is Creator, Redeemer, Sustainer. God is always more than we can grasp. What is important is not that we understand God, but that God understands us. What is important is not that God is omnipresent, omnipotent, but that God is love, the love revealed to us through the person of Jesus

Christ, the love who became incarnate and died on the cross to show us how much God loves us.

God is still a puzzle and always will be. But God forms the central piece in the puzzle of the cross.

Next week we'll look at another part of that puzzle — the puzzle of "Humanity." Amen.

God — General Prayer

O God, King of the universe, mysterious, unfathomable God, we come before you in prayer, bowing before you in wonder and awe. Who are we — weak, sinful human beings — to come before you in prayer? Yet we have come because you have called us. We have come because you have given us the gift of prayer. We have come because you have revealed yourself to us through the person of your Son, Jesus Christ, and have told us to ask, seek, and knock.

So we come to you in prayer, O God, in adoration and worship of you, in contrition and repentance for our sinfulness, and in supplication for the needs of others and for our own needs. Hear our prayers, O God, not because we are worthy, but for the sake of Jesus Christ your only Son, who by his life, death, and resurrection showed us your great love for us. You are mysterious, unfathomable, beyond anything we can comprehend, but above all, you are our Father. For this revelation, we thank and praise you. In that knowledge we come in prayer and pray that prayer your Son taught us to pray, Our Father . . .

Lent 2 — Order of Service

THE PUZZLE OF THE CROSS — HUMANITY

Prelude

Call to Worship: "The Making of Man"
by Priscilla Leonard

Opening Hymn: "Let the Whole Creation Cry"

The First Lesson: Genesis 1:26-31

The Psalmody

The Second Lesson: Romans 8:9-17

Poem: "The Creation"   by James Weldon Johnson

*The Holy Gospel: John 10:31-39

Silent Meditation

The Sermon: "The Puzzle of the Cross — Humanity"

Sermon Hymn: "Just As I Am"

The Offering and Offertory

*Congregational Offertory: The Doxology

*Prayer and Lord's Prayer

*Benediction

Closing Hymn: "Savior Again to Thy Dear Name"

Postlude

*Congregation please stand

2 — Humanity

The Puzzle Of The Cross — Piece Number 2

During these midweek Lenten services we are considering the puzzle of the cross. What makes an ancient instrument of torture and death the symbol of Christianity? Why is it a scandal, a stumbling block to some, but to others, "the power of God and the wisdom of God?" What are the aspects of deity and humanity that go into this makeup?

Last week, we saw that the central piece of the puzzle is God. God is a mystery himself beyond our ability to solve. If God were all alone, there would be no need for a cross. But God is not alone. God created human beings. "Humanity" is the second piece of the puzzle of the cross.

You have already noted where the second piece of the puzzle is placed. It goes in line with the one marked "God." But it is as far from that piece as possible. It is at the bottom of the cross, the part that touches the earth. The puzzle piece of "Humanity" is separated from God, yet points upward to the piece marked "God."

Our psalmody for this evening said, "What is man that thou art mindful of him, and the son of man that thou dost care for him?" What is Man? How does "Humanity" fit into the puzzle of the cross? Humans are very complex beings. In the first place . . .

I. Humans are creaturely

In the second story of creation, found in Genesis 2, we read, "then the Lord God formed man of dust from the ground." We are creatures made out of the dust of the earth. The atoms and molecules that make up our bodies have been around since the day of creation. These same atoms and molecules will return to the earth when we die.

16

In plain truth, we are animals, the very highest order of animals, to be sure, but still animals. Both creation stories bring out the primacy of humans within the order of creation. The first creation story does so by placing the creation of "Humanity" last in the order of animals, and giving humans dominion over "the fish of the sea" and all the other creatures. I especially like that part of having dominion over the fish. I wish the fish knew that.

The second story of creation establishes the primacy of human beings by having the humans created first and the other animals made for the human's pleasure and use. That includes fish, too.

I don't know how you feel about evolution. I personally have no problem with it, for if evolution is the manner in which all creatures came to be, it is God's evolution. Whether we descended from a common ancestor with monkeys, chimpanzees, apes, gorillas or orangutans, or not, the resemblance is still uncanny enough to remind us that we are by nature animals. It may simply be that God has a sense of humor in reminding us of our creatureliness.

Being animals, we experience the basic drives of animals for survival and procreation. We have animal instincts.

I've had people tell me they don't need to go to church; they can find God in nature. It's true, nature does witness to the power and majesty of God, but nature also includes tornados and earthquakes, cancer and illnesses. Nature also displays animals who eat other animals, animals that will even kill their own young, animals whose basic drive is to look out for number one.

Humans are animals. Humans are creatures who have feet of clay. The old liturgy used to declare "We are by nature sinful and unclean." We can say of all "Humanity," male and female, that universally we are creatures.

If that were all that "Humanity" is, there would be no need for a cross, for animals do not sin when they do "what comes naturally." Animals act and react out of instinct. But humans are more than simply animals, creatures:

II. Humans are also spiritual

Humans are different from all the other creatures on earth. Although we may resemble other creatures, like the apes and monkeys, there is a vast difference between us and other creatures. All the others are creatures of habit and instinct. Although evolutionary change may be observed, animals still do what they have done for eons. But, look at humans. We can think and reason. Humans can change their habitats. Humans can think in abstract terms. Humans can express their ideas through language, both oral and written. Just consider the difference between how humans live and how all the other creatures live. Consider housing, food, transportation, communication, and vocation. Think of how differently we live than all other creatures. What makes the difference? Why are we so different?

The difference is spiritual. Humans may have evolved from *homo erectus* to *homo habilus* to *homo sapiens*, but humanity is now *homo spiritus*, the spiritual human. God created humans in his image. This is not a physical image, for the Bible tells us that God is a spirit. The image, therefore, is spiritual. The creation story tells us that "God breathed into his nostrils the breath of life, and man became a living being." Paul wrote, "All who are led by the Spirit of God are sons of God." He wrote, "that we are children of God, and if children then heirs, heirs of God and joint heirs with Christ." I think that is what Jesus was referring to in our gospel lesson for today. Quoting from Psalm 82 Jesus said, "Is it not written, 'I said you are gods'?" If he called them gods to whom the word of God came (and scripture cannot be broken), do you say of him whom the father consecrated and sent into the world, 'You are blaspheming,' because he said 'I am the Son of God?'

We are more than creatures. We are a unique mixture of flesh and spirit. That's where the rub comes. That is where the cross comes. We must decide whether we will live according to self-centeredness or whether we will live according to

God's emphasis on obedience to his will and the good of other people. It is a difference. Paul wrote, "If you live according to the flesh, you will die, but if by the Spirit you put to death the deeds of the body, you will live."

That is where the cross comes in, with its pieces marked "God," "Humanity," "Sin," "Savior," "Sacrifice," and "Salvation." It is through the cross we have access to the Spirit. Paul wrote, "If the spirit of him who raised Jesus from the dead dwells in you, he who raised Christ Jesus from the dead will give life to your mortal bodies also through his Spirit which dwells in you." But there is a cross involved, the cross of Christ and our own crosses that Jesus called us to take up and follow him. Paul wrote that we are children and heirs and fellow heirs with Christ, "provided we suffer with him in order that we may also be glorified with him." There is always the possibility of a cross.

Next week we will look at the third piece of the puzzle. It is called sin. We'll see where that fits into the puzzle of the cross. Amen.

Humanity — General Prayer

O God, King of the universe and our God, we, your human creatures whom you have created in your image, come now before you in prayer. As far as the top of the cross is removed from the bottom, so we creatures are removed from you, the Creator.

O God, this mixture of creature and spirit is so confusing at times. We have urges that well up in us. We have the strong desire to look out for ourselves above the needs of others. We have the desire to be our own boss, to do what we want in total disregard for you or for others.

Yet within us, O God, is that urge, that drive, that tells us "our hearts are restless until they find their rest in thee." You continually call us back to yourself. Help us, O God, to remember who we are and whose we are. Keep the cross before us as we live the life you have given us. Hear us, O God, as we pray the prayer your son taught us to pray, Our Father . . .

Lent 3 — Order of Service

THE PUZZLE OF THE CROSS — SIN

Prelude: "Christe Sanctorum"

Call to Worship: "Judgment and Mercy"   Dorothy L. Sayers

Opening Hymn: "Savior, When in Dust to You"

*Prayer of the Day

The First Lesson: Genesis 3:1-24

Psalmody: Psalm 32

The Second Lesson: Romans 1:18-32

*The Holy Gospel: John 1:29-35

The Sermon: The Puzzle of the Cross — Sin

Sermon Hymn: "Ah, Holy Jesus"

The Offering and Offertory: "God of Grace and God of Glory" Restoration/W. Held

*Congregational Offertory: The Doxology

*Responsive Prayer

*Closing Hymn: "O Sacred Head, Now Wounded"

Postlude

*Benediction

*Congregation please stand

3 — Sin

The Puzzle Of The Cross — Piece Number 3

Here we are, once again, gathered to worship God and consider the puzzle of the cross. By way of review, as they do on the television mini-series, we considered first the piece of the puzzle marked "God." We saw that God is central to the cross, the topmost piece in the puzzle. Last week, we considered the piece marked "Humanity." We saw that human beings are the lowest piece in the puzzle, a unique mixture of flesh and spirit, created in the image of God, but nevertheless creatures.

Tonight, we consider the third piece in the puzzle of the cross, the piece marked "Sin." I have to make a confession. It seems that many ministers are doing that these days. My confession is this: In spite of being trained as a theologian and minister, there is much about the puzzle of God I do not understand. Secondly, since I am one of the genus of animals known as humanity, I do know a little bit about being human. But when it comes to "Sin," I'm an expert. I have my bachelor's, master's, and doctorate in that subject.

There's only one problem: In India we had a delightful proverb to be used in a situation when one person tries to tell another person what they already know, or to describe a situation with which they are already familiar. The proverb says, "It's like teaching your grandfather to cough." There are a lot of us grandfathers and grandmothers here tonight, and we all know how to cough. And all of us, every person in this world, has a doctorate in sinning. Still it behooves us to look at the puzzle of the cross and see where "Sin" fits in.

The display in the narthex and our bulletin cover show that "Sin" is depicted as a triangular-shaped piece that fits right above "Humanity." It shows us what happens when sin comes into our lives.

First of all we need to understand:

I. What "Sin" is

First and foremost, sin is rebellion against God. When God created human beings, he created them in his image. This image is not physical, but spiritual. God created us to be like him. Since God is subject to no one but himself, God has freedom. Since we are made in God's image, we, too, have freedom. We have the freedom to choose. We are not content to be made in God's image. We want to be God. We want to be free, to be answerable to no one, not even God.

The story of Adam and Eve depicts that rebellion. The serpent, the most subtle of all the creatures, tempts Adam and Eve to defy God's command not to eat of the tree of the knowledge of good and evil.

As a result of this rebellion, "Humanity" "missed the mark," went off target, went astray. The Greek word for sin is *harmartia*. It means "to miss the mark."

"Sin" is an inescapable reality in our lives. "We are by nature sinful and unclean." What, then are:

II. The results of "Sin"?

The most serious result is alienation from God. Like the wedge-shaped piece in our puzzle. "Sin" comes between "Humanity" and God. It marks a complete blockage. It looks as though human beings might by dint of their own efforts be able to climb past "Sin" and reach up to God, but it can't be done. "Sin" cuts off the approach.

A military chaplain once asked a group of soldiers if they would like to know whether they were going to heaven or hell. He said he had a little test which would give them the results. They readily agreed, so he gave them some paper and pencils and told them to number down the page 1 to 10. Each question would count ten points. Each soldier was to evalute his or her response on a scale of 1 to 10. He then proceeded to ask the first question. "Have you always loved God above all else and not put anything else before him?" There were other questions about God, family, and conduct as the chaplain went through the Ten Commandments. When the test was over, the chaplain asked them to add up their scores. One man reached 75 and thought that was a good score. It was always a passing grade in school. One man asked, "Padre, what's a passing score for this test?" The chaplain replied, "100 points." Nothing less than perfection can ever earn a way to God. The way is blocked by "Sin." The result is alienation, portrayed in the story of Adam and Eve and their expulsion from the garden and the cherubim and flaming sword that guarded the entrance.

There are other results of "Sin." They are called sins. Paul writes in his letter to the Romans that "God gave them up in the lusts of their heart to impurity, to the dishonoring of their bodies among themselves." He lists a whole catalogue of sins. "They were filled with all manner of wickedness, evil covetousness, malice, full of envy, murder, strife, deceit, malignity. They are gossips, slanderers, haters of God, insolent, haughty, boastful, inventors of evil, disobedient to parents, foolish, faithless, heartless, and ruthless." Paul made a slightly different list for the Christians in Galatia — "immorality, impurity, licentiousness, idolatry, sorcery, enmity, strife, jealousy, anger, selfishness, dissension, party spirit, envy, drunkenness, carousing and the like." All of these Paul terms "works of the flesh." If you had taken that test with the soldiers, what kind of score would you have made? It isn't the cumulative score that counts. The fact is that sins are the result of "Sin," and no one can be reconciled with God by what they do or don't do. No wonder Paul cried out, "Wretched man that I am. Who will deliver me from this body of death?"

We know the answer. It's actually the last three parts of the puzzle. We can't close on this note of hopelessness and despair. Paul knew the answer to his cry. He wrote, "Thanks be to God through Jesus Christ our Lord." John recognized in Jesus what we have come to know by faith. He said, "Behold the Lamb of God, who takes away the sin of the world." We'll be considering for the next three Wednesdays how God did that through Christ.

Before we close, however, let me leave you with this thought: All of us are caught up in "Sin." It's a part of our human nature. It's a part of our nature to be judgmental. It bolsters our ego and our own image of ourselves. We get a kick out of pointing the accusing finger at others, especially if we don't happen to like the other person. We need to remember the result of our own test. It doesn't matter which category we've failed. I would venture to say we fail in all of them. The result is the same. The result of sin is alienation. All of us stand under God's righteous condemnation. Let me leave with you the thought contained in this poem by John Byrom called "Self-righteousness."

> *"He is a sinner," you are pleased to say.*
> *Then love him for the sake of Christ, I pray.*
> *If on His gracious words you place your trust,*
> *"I came to call sinners, not the just."*
> *Second His call: which if you will not do,*
> *You'll be the greater sinner of the two.*

God grant that we may remember who we are and who Christ is and forgive others as we are forgiven. Amen.

Sin — General Prayer

O God our heavenly Father, as we come before you in prayer, we come with a deep sense of the burden of sin that weighs us down and stands as barrier between us and you. It is a barrier that we cannot remove, because in our creatureliness we are too weak to do so. Unless you take away our sin, we are forever alienated from you.

Even though we are only halfway through the puzzle of the cross, we know, Lord, that you have done something to remove that barrier. You sent your son, and he died on the cross for us. Words cannot express what that means for us. Help us, Lord, to respond with the gift of our love and devotion. Help us to conquer the urges that often threaten to overwhelm us. Help us to turn our lives over to your control. Be with us, that in all that we do, we may do to your honor and glory. This we ask in the name and for the sake of him who gave his life for us, even our Lord Jesus Christ, who taught us to say when we pray, Our Father . . .

Lent 4 — Order of Service

THE PUZZLE OF THE CROSS — SAVIOR

Organ Prelude: "My Soul Exults the Lord"   J. S. Bach

Call to Worship: "I Know A Name"   Author Unknown

Opening Hymn: "Beautiful Savior"

*Prayer of the Day

The First Lesson: Isaiah 49:1-6

The Psalmody: Psalm 30

The Second Lesson: Acts 2:14-39

*The Holy Gospel: John 1:1-18

The Sermon: The Puzzle of the Cross — Savior

Sermon Hymn: "Beneath the Cross of Jesus"

The Offering and Offertory: "My Soul Exults the Lord"
Marcel Dupre

*Congregational Offertory: The Doxology

*Prayer and Lord's Prayer

*Benediction

*Closing Hymn: "In the Hour of Trial"

Postlude

*Congregation please stand

4 — Savior

The Puzzle Of The Cross — Piece Number 4

We're more than halfway through putting the pieces of the puzzle of the cross into place. Since there are only six pieces, it isn't difficult to figure out. A few people told me they had taken one of the flyers we distributed beforehand, cut out the pieces and solved the puzzle ahead of time. They jokingly said they didn't have to come on Wednesday evenings, since they already had the puzzle solved. I hope they said it in jest. Solving the puzzle of the cross involves more than just putting the pieces of the puzzle we supplied in their proper places.

Solving the puzzle would have been a lot harder if we didn't already know the shape it was to form, the shape of the cross.

Suppose you were given the six pieces of the puzzle and told to put them together without knowing what form they were to take? It would be like trying to work a picture puzzle without any of the border pieces or a picture showing what the puzzle would look like. You could put the six pieces of the puzzle together in any number of possible combinations.

Then, suppose that at first only three parts of the puzzle were labeled, those marked "God," "Humanity," and "Sin." You might figure out that "Humanity" and "Sin" fit together, since we are so sinful. You could surmise that "God" would be above "Humanity" and "Sin," probably with "Sin" in between, but how would you join them together? Some other pieces are needed.

We need to remember that the situation of the Jewish faith was something like that. God had revealed himself as the Holy One, the one true God, a mystery in himself. He seemed to them to have become almost inaccessible in his utter holiness. He had revealed to them that they had been created in his image and were meant to be in communion with him. But they also knew that "Sin" had come into the world because of their creaturely selfishness and had become a barrier between God and them. They knew instinctively that something had to be done to effect a reconciliation between God and them. They developed an intricate system of offerings and sacrifices to appease God and earn his forgiveness. Some of them even began to sense that this reconciliation went beyond life on this earth to include eternal life with God. They began to see that a piece of the puzzle was called "Salvation." But what were the other two pieces?

In the fullness of time, God began to reveal to them through his holy prophets that a central piece of the puzzle was labeled "Savior." This was the anointed one, the messiah, the Christ. This messiah was to be a human being in the same form as "Humanity." He would be their deliverer. There were several problems involved, however. First of all, they did not have an exact description of this messiah. Various prophets had written at different times and under differing circumstances. Some wrote of the messiah as a conquering hero, driving out all the enemies of Israel and providing them with a pure theocratic state with the messiah as their king. Some wrote of the messiah as a suffering servant, undergoing terrible pain and affliction in order to redeem Israel.

Another problem was that they did not know when the messiah was to come. The prophets had foretold some of the signs of the time, but there were many times in their history that would have satisfied these conditions. They could not know the time, the *Kairotic* time of God's plan.

There had been false messiahs who had coerced people to believe in them and follow them, only to see them fail and their followers killed.

I think this kind of understanding helps us not to be so judgmental toward the Jews of Jesus' day, or even the Jews of our day, for it is not all that easy to understand. One of our great Lutheran leaders (I forget whether it was Franklin Clark Fry or Oswald Hoffman) once said, "If I had lived at the time of Jesus, I probably would have helped to crucify him." I suspect that some of us would have done the same.

It is only from the vantage point of history that we can see how all the pieces of the puzzle of the messiah fell into place. Even the disciples with their ringside seats could not understand what was happening until after the resurrection. Then the piece of the puzzle marked "Savior" fell into place. Then Peter could stand before the people on the day of Pentecost and recite a brief outline of the holy history that had led up to the crucifixion and resurrection of Jesus the Christ, the messiah.

Now we can see with the eyes of faith the picture of the Christ, the messiah, as the suffering servant who is also the conquering king. Now we see that the messiah's kingdom consists of more than the tribes of Jacob, and that God has sent his servant Son "as the light to the nations . . . that salvation may reach to the end of the earth." Now we can understand that God made a new covenant with his people, a covenant whose symbol is the cross, whose seal is the blood of the Lamb, whose effect is to join all the pieces of the puzzle together, as it is to join all people together beneath the cross of Jesus. Our first lesson this coming Sunday is from the book of Jeremiah and speaks more of this new covenant. The gospel lesson for this Sunday begins with some Greeks coming to Philip and saying, "Sir, we would see Jesus." Often as I enter the pulpit I am reminded of those words: "Sir, we would see Jesus." All of us need to see Jesus. Every person in the world needs to see Jesus.

The salvation of this planet and all who live on it does not depend on economics or politics or military might. It does not depend on treaties made by people. The salvation of this world and all who live on it depends on the covenant God has made with us through his son, Jesus Christ. That is why the church has such a vital part to play in the history and salvation of "Humanity." That is why there is such an urgency for Christians at all levels of life to share the good news of the gospel with others. And we need to proclaim the same gospel to ourselves, too, for all of us need its blessed assurance daily. Anna B. Warner wrote a poem titled "Let Us See Jesus."

We would see Jesus — for the shadows lengthen
Across the little landscape of our life;
We would see Jesus — our weak faith to strengthen,
For the last weariness, the final strife.

We would see Jesus — other lights are paling,
Which for long years we have rejoiced to see;
The blessings of our pilgrimage~are failing,
We would not mourn them, for we come to thee.

We would see Jesus — the great rock-foundation
Whereon our feet are set by sovereign grace!
Nor life, nor death, with all their agitation,
Can't thence remove us, if we see his face.

We would see Jesus — that is all we're needing,
Strength, joy and willingness come with the sight;
We would see Jesus — dying, risen, pleading —
Then welcome day, and farewell mortal night.

Anna B. Warner, 1820-1915

Next week we will consider what it cost our Lord that we might see him. Amen.

Savior — General Prayer

O God, our heavenly Father, once again we come to you in prayer. Unworthy sinners though we are, still we come before you. We worship and adore you, O God, for you are our creator, the creator of all that exists in this vast universe. We are overwhelmed by the vastness of creation and our own finiteness. We are further overwhelmed when we remember our sinful condition and know that this sinfulness forms a barrier between us and you.

How thankful we are, Father, that your great love for us caused you to send us a savior, your son, Jesus Christ. We rejoice that he has done what we cannot do, by removing our sin from us and making it possible for us to come to you. May we ever respond with our love and devotion, Lord, and may we reach out to others with the good news of your love.

During this lenten season, and throughout our lives, keep the cross before our eyes, that we may never forget what it cost you to save us from our sin. This we ask in the name and for the sake of him who came to be our savior, even Jesus Christ our Lord who taught us to pray, Our Father . . .

Lent 5 — Order of Service

THE PUZZLE OF THE CROSS — SACRIFICE

Prelude: "Sacred Harp Suite"   Organ
(Do Not I Love Thee, O My Lord) I, II, III, R. J. Powell

Call to Worship: Psalm 22:1-23

Opening Hymn: "Jesus, I Will Ponder Now"

*Prayer of the Day

The First Lesson: Isaiah 53:1-12

The Second Lesson: 1 Corinthians 1:18-25

*The Holy Gospel: Mark 14:53—15:15

The Sermon: The Puzzle of the Cross — Sacrifice

Sermon Hymn: "Alas, And Did My Savior Bleed"

The Offering and Offertory: "Sacred Harp Suite"
        (Do Not I Love Thee, O My Lord) IV, R. J. Powell

*Congregational Offertory: The Doxology

*Responsive Prayer

*Closing Hymn: "Deep Were His Wounds"

Postlude: "Scared Harp Suite"
        (Do Not I Love Thee, O My Lord) V, R. J. Powell

*Congregation please stand

5 — Sacrifice

The Puzzle Of The Cross — Piece Number 5

The puzzle is almost complete. Only one more piece to go. It wasn't hard to guess where this next-to-last piece goes, was it? Not hard to place, but awfully hard to understand.

We keep finding puzzles within the puzzle. We noted the puzzle of God that still exists and will exist because our finite minds cannot encompass the infinite God. We noted the puzzle "Humanity," this strange mixture of creature and spirit, this mixture of male and female, this wonderful inner longing to be in communion with God and this horrible rebellion against God as we strive to be our own boss. We considered the puzzle of the "Savior," that glorious mixture of conquering king and suffering servant. Here in the flesh is God incarnate, God come to earth to reconcile "Humanity" to himself.

Tonight we contemplate how God brought about that reconciliation through "Sacrifice." Here again is another puzzle. How does it work? What does the death of a young Jewish carpenter-turned-preacher on a cross 2,000 years ago have to do with our salvation? Why did Jesus have to die on the cross? How can the incarnate son sacrifice his life to the eternal Father?

Perhaps it will help us to understand the puzzle of "Sacrifice" if we remember that the cross stands at the crossroads of time. The cross marks the completion of the old covenant and the inception of the new covenant. Let us look at "Sacrifice" from the viewpoint of:

I. The Old Covenant

Last Sunday we saw that the old covenant as outlined by Moses followed closely the common formula of ancient covenants made between a conquering king and his subjugated vassals. These ancient covenants were marked by the ceremonial shedding of blood by slaughtering an animal.

Even before Moses completed the ratification of the old covenant, the ritual of animal sacrifice existed. God was conceived as being a jealous God, a God of wrath and vengeance. You had to stay on the good side of God. The only way to do that was to make a sacrifice. Since it was thought that the soul force lay in the blood, then blood had to be shed. It was written, "Without the shedding of blood, there is no forgiveness of sin."

The result of this was an elaborate system of sacrifices. The size of the sacrifice was in proportion to the size of the sin. Since God is holy and pure, only the best could be sacrificed. The Old Testament is full of descriptions and regulations concerning how sacrifice is to be carried out.

Looking at the sacrifice of our Lord from the viewpoint of the old covenant, we see the completion, the final sacrifice, under this system. Here is the Paschal Lamb, the perfect, sinless Lamb of God, who is sacrificed to God on behalf of our sin. By the shedding of his blood, we are washed in the blood of the Lamb. The book of Hebrews deals at length with this concept of the old covenant. In it we see not only the perfect sacrifice, but Jesus, who is also the perfect, sinless high priest, who makes the necessary sacrifice of himself once and for all. It truly is finished. There is no longer any need for animal sacrifices. The old covenant is finished.

But there is another aspect to this piece of the puzzle. We need to look at "Sacrifice" from the viewpoint of:

II. The New Covenant

The new covenant reveals to us, not a God of wrath and vengeance who must be appeased, but a God of love who gives his Son. We get glimmerings of this God in the Old Testament. In Psalm 51 the psalmist wrote, "You take no delight in burntofferings. The sacrifice of God is a troubled spirit, a broken and contrite heart, O God you will not despise." Jesus

35

demonstrated his disdain for all the ritual and petty laws that got in the way of the people understanding their true relationship to God.

It was inevitable that such a radical change would produce a backlash. It was a terrible series of physical punishments our Lord endured in obedience to the will of the Father. Jesus knew that his continued proclamation of the kingdom of God with its message of relationship rather than ritual would result in his ultimate death. He saw this in terms of the covenant relationship. The new covenant would also be sealed with a sacrifice, a sacrifice not of an animal, a sacrifice not made in appeasement, a sacrifice not between a vassal and his king, but a sacrifice of the only begotten son, a sacrifice made in love, a sacrifice of God to God. Still a puzzle to our finite minds, but one we must accept in faith, for our Lord told us, "This is my body, given for you . . . This is the blood of the New Covenant shed for you and for many for the remission of sin."

It is no wonder our Lord prayed in the garden that the Father might take his cup of suffering from him. We often forget the extent of that suffering. Our scriptures rather quickly pass over the punishment Jesus received from the hands of his captors. Our lesson reported, "And some began to spit on him . . . and to strike him . . . and the guards received him with blows." Then a little further on we read, "And having scourged Jesus, he delivered him to be crucified." Much of the suffering our Lord received occurred before he was crucified.

I recently finished reading a book on the Shroud of Turin, a fascinating scientific study of this religious relic. Some scientists are certain that it is the linen cloth in which our Lord was buried. The image on that shroud shows the face of a man who had been beaten badly. His eyes were swollen, his nose had been broken, and patches of his beard had been pulled out by the roots. His scalp was lacerated by many wounds that had bled freely. His back and the upper portion of his legs were a mass of open wounds and small depressions left by the

Roman flaggelum, a short-handled whip of thongs which were tipped by small lead dumbbells and pieces of sharp bone. Many people died simply of the scourging. The shoulders reveal the chafing marks of a heavy burden carried after the scourging. One knee is deeply gashed, probably from a fall while carrying the burden. There are wound marks in the wrists and feet where nails had been driven. There are streaks of blood on the arms in two directions, as the victim alternately slumped upon the cross in agony and pain and then had to try to stand erect in order to be able to breathe. Finally, there is the mark of a large wound made by a spear that pierced the heart.

Only the last part of our Lord's sacrifice was on the cross. His blood was sprinkled in the house of Caiaphas, in the Fortress of Antonia and along the Via Dolorosa. His was truly a bloody sacrifice.

The Romans were not interested in painless and swift executions. They were not bothered by the concept of cruel and unusual punishment. Their object was not only to punish the offender but to warn others. The cross was one of the most horrible types of executions. It was reserved only for non-Romans. Because of what Christ did for us on the cross, we have made it the symbol of our faith. Let us never forget what it cost our Lord to make that sacrifice. Let us never forget that his sacrifice resulted in our salvation. That part of the puzzle, the final part, we shall consider next week. Amen.

Sacrifice — General Prayer

O God, our heavenly Father, as we come to you in prayer, we stand in the shadow of the cross. With the eye of faith we see our Lord hanging on that cross, a bloody sacrifice for our sins. Like Luther, we cannot fathom how you could die on the cross. What we can grasp in a human way is how very much you must love us to allow your son to die on the cross for us. We are not worthy of your love, Father. We are sinners who justly deserve your condemnation, but we thank and praise you for your love, and for the gift of salvation that comes through the cross.

Grant, O Lord, that we might be moved to show your love for others through the sacrifices we make for others. Help us always to seek to do your will, as our Lord did. Help us to be willing to sacrifice ourselves in the service of others.

We commend ourselves into your loving care, asking you to watch over us, guide us, and use us in your service. This we ask in the name of Jesus Christ, who taught us to pray, Our Father . . .

Maundy Thursday — Order of Service

Prelude

*Invocation

*Hymn: "In the Cross of Christ I Glory"

*Prayer

Psalmody

The First Lesson: Exodus 24:3-11

The Second Lesson: 1 Corinthians 10:16-21

*The Holy Gospel: Mark 14:12-26

The Sermon: The Puzzle of the Cross — Salvation

Prayer of Confession and Absolution

Communion Hymn

The Offering and Offertory

*Offering Prayer

*The Great Thanksgiving

*Words of Institution

*Lord's Prayer

The Communion

*Post Communion

Hymn: "One There Is Above All Others"

Stripping of the Altar

Postlude

*Congregation please stand

6 — Salvation

The Puzzle Of The Cross — Piece Number 6

We have been considering the puzzle of the cross. We have put the puzzle together piece-by-piece, observing the position of each piece and contemplating the relationship of one piece to another. We have seen how there is a natural progression to the pieces of the puzzle as we consider the pieces labeled "God," "Humanity," "Sin," "Savior," and "Sacrifice."

Tonight we put the last piece into place, the piece marked "Salvation." The puzzle is complete. We have the shape of the cross. Without that final piece, the puzzle makes no sense. Without the cross, there is no salvation. Through the cross, the connection between God and man is re-established. That is "Salvation." That is why the cross stands as a symbol for Christianity, why an instrument of pain and death has become the symbol of healing and life.

We deal with symbols in the church because we cannot portray the mystical relationship between ourselves and God without using symbols. Though we have "solved" the puzzle of the cross, we have seen that there are still many puzzles in life and in our relationship to God, the greatest puzzle of all.

In the church we have two other symbols for "Salvation." We call them sacraments. We Lutherans define a sacrament as that which has the command of Christ, the promise of God, and the symbol of an earthly element. There are two sacraments, baptism and holy communion. One reminds us of birth, the new life by the washing of regeneration. The symbol is water. The command is "Go and baptize." The promise is eternal life. The other reminds us of death, the breaking of the body and the shedding of blood. The symbol is bread and wine. The command is "Take and eat . . . take and drink." The promise is eternal life. Both point to the gracious gift of salvation, the washing away of our sin and the newness of life in Christ.

What a puzzle it must have been that evening when Jesus transformed the celebration of the passover meal into the celebration of the holy supper, the eucharist, the communion. For centuries the passover had been celebrated in remembrance of their delivery out of slavery in Egypt into the promised land. The observance had developed a by-the-number ritual. They had carefully chosen a spotless lamb and sacrificed it in the temple, throwing some of the blood on the altar. They had dutifully smeared the doorposts of their homes with blood as they had done in Egypt so the Angel of the Lord would pass over them. They had cooked all the traditional foods and eaten them in the prescribed manner. They had drunk the prescribed number of glasses of diluted wine. They had set an empty place in the hopes that Elijah would return as the scriptures foretold.

But suddenly the disciples are confronted with a puzzle, with a mystery. Jesus says to them, as he takes the bread and blesses and breaks it. "Take, this is my body," and as he takes a cup of wine, gives thanks and says, "This is the blood of the covenant which is poured out for many." They had heard Jesus tell them several times that he must go up to Jerusalem and suffer and die, but they just couldn't grasp it. It took the cross to help them solve the puzzle. It took the cross and the resurrection. It took the empty cross and the empty tomb and the revelation of a risen Christ to solve the puzzle. Then they realized who had been among them. Then they realized that they, like Moses and Aaron, Nadab and Abihu and the seventy elders, had seen the God of Israel. They had "beheld God, and ate and drank."

We have gathered here this evening in commemoration of that first Maundy Thursday. We gather in the shadow of the cross. Although there is still mystery involved, we understand more completely the puzzle of the cross. We understand that through the sacrifice of his life on the cross we receive the gift of salvation. In this cup of blessing we participate in the blood of Christ. In this bread which we break, we participate in the body of Christ. We cannot explain how Christ comes to us again in the bread and wine. It is only bread and wine, but when it is accompanied by the command of Christ, "Take and eat . . . take and drink," when it touches our lips and is taken into our bodies, we receive Christ anew in our hearts.

Much of life is still a puzzlement. It can be such a mixture of joy and sorrow, triumph and defeat, contentment and frustration. Some day, when we see it from the perspective of heaven, we will understand the puzzle completely. For now, let us put our trust and faith in Christ, confident that he will guide us and be with us through all the puzzles of life and will someday receive us into heaven to be with him eternally. Amen.

Salvation — General Prayer

O God, the picture puzzle of the cross is now complete, but we still cannot understand all the mysteries, the puzzle of faith. We are surrounded by mysteries, Lord, but we rejoice because they are your mysteries. Even though we cannot know you completely, we rejoice that you know us through and through, and, in spite of knowing us to be sinners, you love us with such a deep and abiding love.

As we draw near to the end of this lenten season, may we be drawn nearer to you. Help us to keep the cross before us, not only in lent, but every day of our lives. Help us to feel the power of your love as it reaches us through our savior and overcomes sin by his sinless and selfless sacrifice, so that we may experience the joy of your salvation.

For these times of gathering beneath the cross of Jesus, we give you thanks and praise, through your son, Jesus Christ, who taught us to pray, Our Father . . .

Suggested Hymns

I — God

"My God How Wonderful Thou Art"
"Immortal, Invisible, God Only Wise"
"Holy God, We Praise Thy Name"
"How Great Thou Art"
"A Mighty Fortress"
"Holy, Holy, Holy! Lord God Almighty"
"God of Our Life"
"Now Thank We All Our God"

II — Humanity

"Just As I Am"
"Savior Again to Thy Dear Name"
"My Faith Looks up to Thee"
"Have Thine Own Way, Lord"
"Take Up Thy Cross"
"O Master, Let Me Walk with Thee"
"Make Me a Captive, Lord"
"Take My Life, and Let It Be Consecrated"

III — Sin

"Savior, When in Dust to You"
"Ah, Holy Jesus"
"O Sacred Head, Now Wounded"
"There Is a Green Hill Far Away"
"When I Survey the Wondrous Cross"
"Rescue the Perishing"
"Make Me a Captive, Lord"
"There Is a Balm in Gilead"

IV — Savior

"Beautiful Savior"
"Beneath the Cross of Jesus"
"In the Hour of Trial"
"In the Cross of Christ I Glory"
"There Is a Fountain Filled with Blood"
"Jesus, Keep Me Near the Cross"
"There's a Wideness in God's Mercy"
"Jesus, the Very Thought of Thee"

V — Sacrifice

"Jesus, I Will Ponder Now"
"Alas! And Did My Savior Bleed"
"Deep Were His Wounds"
"Go to Dark Gethsemane"
"Were You There?"
"What Wondrous Love Is This"
"Behold the Savior of Mankind"
"Cross of Jesus, Cross of Sorrow"

VI — Salvation

"Jesus Shall Reign"
"All Hail the Power of Jesus' Name"
"Thou Art the Way; to Thee Alone"
"Take the Name of Jesus with You"
"Amazing Grace! How Sweet the Sound"
"Art Thou Weary, Art Thou Languid"
"One There Is Above All Others"
"They'll Know We are Christians By Our Love"

Acknowledgements

The following poems are published in this book by permission from Harper and Row Publishers, Inc. New York. The poems were published in "Masterpieces of Religious Verse," edited by James Dalton Morrison and published by Harper Brothers Publishers, 1948.

"Self-Righteousness," by John Byrom (1692-1763)

"Let Us See Jesus," by Anna B. Warner (1820-1915)

"The Great Voice," by Clinton Scollard (1860-1932)

Cross Puzzle Display Instructions

During your Lenten series on "The Puzzle of the Cross" you may wish to design a cross puzzle for display in your church. The following grid can be used to create such a puzzle. By using the grid you can make a cross of any size. You may use any material you choose for the background and for the cross. The words used on the cross puzzle relate to the sermon titles in this series.

Churches also have that opportunity to create individual cross puzzle pieces as handouts to members. In this way, members may take home and construct their own cross puzzle. Each piece of the puzzle is labeled in relation to the sermon titles in this series. A cross puzzle packet is available from C.S.S. The packet is number 9111-X.

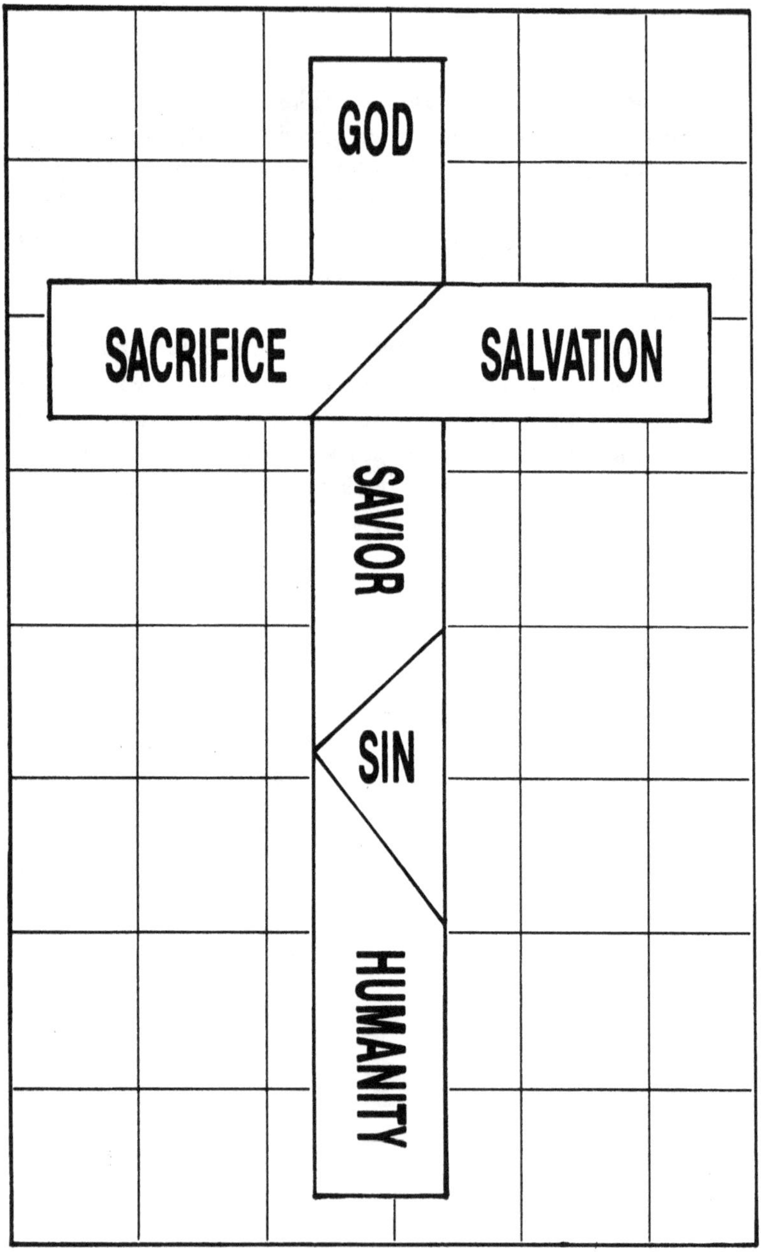
GOD
SACRIFICE
SALVATION
SAVIOR
SIN
HUMANITY